THE AFRICAN AMERICAN COLLECTION

CECIL COUNTY
MARYLAND

Indentures

1777-1814

Jerry M. Hynson

HERITAGE BOOKS
2007

HERITAGE BOOKS
AN IMPRINT OF HERITAGE BOOKS, INC.

Books, CDs, and more—Worldwide

For our listing of thousands of titles see our website
at
www.HeritageBooks.com

Published 2007 by
HERITAGE BOOKS, INC.
Publishing Division
65 East Main Street
Westminster, Maryland 21157-5026

Other books by the author:

Absconders, Runaways and Other Fugitives in the Baltimore City and County Jail

Baltimore Life Insurance Company Genealogical Abstracts

District of Columbia Runaway and Fugitive Slave Cases, 1848-1863

Free African-Americans, Maryland 1832: Including Allegany, Anne Arundel, Calvert, Caroline, Cecil, Charles, Dorchester, Frederick, Kent, Montgomery, Queen Anne's, and St. Mary's Counties

Maryland Freedom Papers, Volume 1: Anne Arundel County

Maryland Freedom Papers, Volume 2: Kent County

Maryland Freedom Papers, Volume 3: Maryland Colonization Society Manumission Book, 1832-1860

The African American Collection: Anne Arundel County, Maryland Marriage Licenses, 1865-1888

The African American Collection: Kent County, Maryland Marriages , 1865-1888

International Standard Book Number: 978-0-7884-4112-4

Cecil County Maryland – Indentures

Contents

Introduction

The apprentice system of training youth in useful vocations has a long history in Maryland. The system provided for solutions for two social problems. First, it assured the continuous development of a body of skilled artisans to perform the daily tasks and services required to keep the daily needs of the community fulfilled. A continuous supply of carpenters, blacksmiths, wheel makers, and other such occupations flowed from this system. In addition, the need to provide for the daily requirements of food, clothing, and supervision of orphans and other unsupervised and unskilled youth were met through this system which has existed since the earliest days of the settlement of Maryland. It should be noted that with some modification, the apprenticeship continues to serve us in fields such as electrical services, tool and die making, plumbing, and architecture.

Early apprenticeships were governed under the jurisdiction of 'trustees of the poor', a select group of citizens appointed by the governor or the state assembly. In some jurisdictions administration was placed in the hands of the local justices of the peace. As the system expanded jurisdiction was moved to the Orphans Courts. Trustees, justices, and courts oversaw the apprenticeship system under legislation from the General Assembly.

The administration of the apprentice system resulted in the formation of a body of records holding invaluable information for the genealogical researcher. These records are found in separate bound volumes containing the records of the Orphans Courts of Maryland. In some cases the records are intermingled with the Property Records of a jurisdiction with the deeds and property sales documents.

The information contained in the records is invaluable. In most instances the name of apprentice, the name of the master, the date of initiation of the apprenticeship, the term of apprenticeship, and the vocation to be taught can be found. Some cases also give the name of at least one parent or guardian of the apprentice. In many cases the location of the apprenticeship in terms of a political district is given.

This volume is an attempt to present a summary of the Apprentice cases in Cecil County, Maryland from 1777 until 1805. The records are formatted in the following manner: the name of the apprentice, accompanied by any parental information found; the birth date of the apprentice; the age of the apprentice; the name of the Master and trade if known; beginning date of the apprenticeship; and the length of time to be served. In some cases the age of the apprentice determines when the contract is concluded. In the case of males, a contract was generally concluded when the apprentice attained the age of 21. For females the concluding condition was either attainment of age 16 or marriage subject to the approval of the master.

LAWS OF MARYLAND

CHAP. XXI. [1]
An ACT to enlarge the powers of the trustees of the poor of the several counties therein mentioned.

BE it enacted, *by the General Assembly of Maryland,* That from and after this session of assembly, any three trustees of the poor in each of the several counties on the eastern shore of this state, be and they are hereby constituted a sufficient board to transact any business as trustees of the poor for their several counties, and that any business done by three trustees, met together by appointment for the transacting of business as aforesaid, shall be as valid as if done by the whole of the said trustees, any law heretofore made to the contrary
notwithstanding.

II. And be it enacted, That it shall and may be lawful for the trustees as aforesaid, or any three of them, to bind out any orphans under their care in said poor-house, to any discreet person applying for said orphan or orphans, always having a regard to give a preference to tradesmen and mechanics, by obliging said applicants for said orphan or orphans to sign a good and sufficient indenture to learn said apprentice the occupation that he follows, and to find him in good sufficient clothing, meat, drink, washing and lodging, and to give such education as masters are obliged to give to apprentices bound by the several county courts of this state; and said indenture, when so taken, shall be lodged with the clerk of the county where such indenture is taken, by any one of the trustees of the poor of said county, within thirty days after the execution thereof, under the penalty of three pounds for every neglect, to be recovered by presentment in the county court of the county where any such orphan shall be bound, and

[1] Web Site: Maryland State Archives
Publication: Archives of Maryland, Laws of Maryland , Chapter XXI, Vol. 204 - 1785-1791, pp. 555-556

applied to the use and benefit of the poor of said county; and the clerk of said county shall and he is hereby obliged to receive and record the said indenture as other indentures heretofore taken for orphans bound by the court of said county, and the said clerk shall be allowed the sum of three shillings current money for each

and every indenture so received and recorded, to be assessed in the levy of said county.

III.   And be it enacted, That if any of the trustees of the poor of the counties aforesaid shall neglect to attend on any the days appointed by the trustees for the meeting of said trustees, and transacting of business, it shall and may be lawful for the said trustees, or any three of them, when met as aforesaid, to proceed to fine such person or persons so neglecting to attend, in any sum not exceeding ten shillings for every such neglect, to be applied as aforesaid.

References

Cecil, Charles, Frederick (Counties)
1806 – 1863 (Indentures, Certificates of Freedom)
MSA CR 47246
Maryland State Archives
350 Rowe Boulevard
Annapolis, Md.

Archives of Maryland (electronic edition)
Maryland State Archives Internet Web Site
Mdarchives.state.md.us?subject=Volume 000068
Maryland State Archives
350 Rowe Boulevard
Annapolis, Md.

234

Darcus Wilson

Cecil County

This Indenture made this eighth Day of January in the year of our Lord Eighteen hundred and five, witnesseth that John Groome, and John King, two Justices of the peace for the County aforesaid, have and by these presents do put, place and bind Darcus Wilson, being an Orphan Girl of said County, unto George Bains Shoemaker, of the said County, and with him after the manner of a Apprentice to live from the Day of the Date hereof, until she arrives at the age of Sixteen years she being thirteen years of age on the seventeenth Day of March last past. And the same Master shall teach or cause the said Apprentice to be taught to read and write, and be brought up in the Christian Religion and shall also teach her or cause her to be taught the Art, Mistery, Business, Trade, or Occupation of Housekeeping.

That the said Apprentice shall in all things lawfully, well, and faithfully, serve her said Master and do the same to the utmost of her power: And the said Apprentice to be in all things used and dealt with according to the form of an Act of assembly entitled "an Act for the regulation of Apprentices". And last, the said Master, shall find and provide his said Apprentice, during the time of her Apprenticeship, with sufficient meat, drink, washing, lodging, and apparel, both linnen and wollen, neat and convenient for such a Apprentice: And shall also give his said Apprentice at the expiration of her time aforesaid, besides the common wearing apparel one new suit of apparel. &c

In testimony whereof the parties aforesaid have hereunto set their hands and seals the Day and year above written.

Sealed and Delivered
in presence of

Tobias Rudolph

John Groome (Seal)
John King (Seal)
George Bains (Seal)

Huggins, Mary, daughter of Samuel; 19 March 1783; 11; Magee, James; 10 May 1794; to serve until 16

Duncan, John; 1 November 1784; 9; Wallace, Michael Dr.; 10 June 1794; to serve until 21

Younger, James, son of Hannah; 7 February 1787; 7; Wallace, Michael Dr; 10 June 1794; to serve until 21

Bulteel, Rachel, daughter of Henry; 20 March 1781; 13; Whan, Sally Mrs.; 12 August 1794; to serve until 16

Mills, Robert of John; 25 August 1779; 15; McGrady, John, tanner; 12 August 1794; to serve until 21

Brown, Joseph, son of John; 11 April 1778; 16; Miles, Isaac, blacksmith; 22 August 1794; to serve until 21

Harridge, Samuel, son of Mary (deceased) of Lancaster, Pennsylvania; 1777; - ; Campbell, John, Taylor; 30 August 1794; to serve until 21

Bavington, William, son of Richard; 10 August 1780; 14; Bane, Nathan, blacksmith; 15 October 1794; to serve until 21

Money, Robert, son of Hyland; 1 February 1777; 17;

Jackson, Henry, shoemaker; 15 October 1794; to serve until 21

Parry, Sarah, daughter of David; 27 October 1782; 12; Oldham, Richard; 9 December 1794; TBF at age 16

McCrakin, Thomas Blair, son of James; 30 August 1780; 15; Bennett, John, taylor; 10 February 1795; to serve until age 21

Pennington, William, son of Isaac; 5 March 1782; 12; Ryland, Peter, farmer; 10 February 1795; to serve until 21

Negro Abigal, daughter of Judith; 1 January 1782; 13; Bond, Abel; 10 February 1795; to serve until 16

Gilbeath, William, son of James Gilbeath; 18; Brown, Elisha, cooper; 29 November 1794; to serve 2 years, 9 months

Hendricks, Jacob, son of Elizabeth; 20 December 1794; 14; Terry, William, cooper; 29 November 1794; to serve until age 21

Wright, Thomas; 1896; 9; Sharpe, John, cooper; 4 March 1795; to serve until age 21

Sparrowgrow, John, son of Lydia; 20 September 1794; 12; Moore, George, farmer;

14 April 1795; to serve until age 21

Bennett, John, son of Millicent; 1 April 1791; 4; Samuel Mittes/Mitter; 15 April 1795; to serve until age 21

Wyncoop, Abraham; - ; - ; Chandler, Francis B.; 9 April 1795; TBF 4 years hence

Parry, Jesse, son of David; 3 May 1789; 6; Brown, Jesse, blacksmith; 10 June 1795; TBF@ age 21

Hammond, John, son of Poll, a free mulatto; 1 May 1751; 14; Anderson, Samuel, husbandman; - ; to serve until age 21

Glenn, Samuel Jr., son of Joannes (deceased); 1758; 17; Hollingsworth, Henry, Tanner; 24 June 1895; to serve until age 21

Watts, Samuel, son of Catherine Watts; 1 February 1785; 10; Winchester, William, husbandman; 24 June 1795; to serve until age 21

Davison, Robert, son of Sussanah; 21 October 1785; 9; McGrady, John, Sadler; 14 October 1795; to serve until age 21

Davison, Margaret, daughter of Sussanah; 19 August 1783; 12; McGrady, John, Sadler;

14 October 1795; to serve until age 16

Money, Thomas, son of Eleanor; 4 December 1781; 14; Edmiston, David, husbandman; 8 December 1795; to serve until age 21

Winchester, Timothy, son of Ann; 6 February 1791; 3; Edmiston, David, husbandman; 8 December 1795; to serve until age 21

Bird, John, son of Thomas Bird; - ; - ; Arthur, James, house carpenter; 19 August 1795; to serve six years, 5 months then free

Knott, James, son of William Knott; 15 September 1777; 18; Conway, William, refiner of iron; 8 April 1796; to serve two years, 10 months, then free

Martin, Hester; 1787; 8; Owens, Thomas; 8 March 1796; to serve until 16, then free

Jones, Richard; 18 March 1786; 10; Wilson, Isaac, farmer; 12 April 1796; to serve until 21

Shaw, John; 1782; 14; Thompson, William, shoemaker; 8 April 1796; to serve 5 years, eight months, seven days

Lashley, Thomas; 1782; 14; Allen, Captain John (Bay Captain); 12 April 1796; to serve 6 years, eight months, 14 days

Hyatt, Abraham, son of Abraham; 6 July 1792; 4; Bing, Oliver, mason and bricklayer; 4 May 1796; to serve until age 21

Bird, Elizabeth; 1791; 5; Archibald, David; 14 June 1796; to serve until age 16

Sullivan, William; 1790; 5; England, John, weaver; 14 June 1796; to serve until age 21

Sullivan, Rebecca; 1792; 3; England, John, weaver; 14 June 1796; to serve until 16

Campbell, Samuel; 1779; 17; Reynolds, Thomas; 14 June 1796; to serve until 21

Crowley, John of John; 23 March 1785; 11; Miller, Samuel, farmer; 15 June 1796; to serve until 21

Lancaster, Isaac; 24 November 1780; 15; Jackson, Peter, weaver; 15 June 1796; to serve until 21

Pennington, Elias, mulatto; 1795; 9; Pearce, Henry Ward; 30 July 1796; to serve until 21

Wirt, John, son of Jacob; 1 March 1782; 14; Miller, Lewis; 9 August 1796; to serve until 21

Lowe, Levi, of Elizabeth Badger; 3 May 1781; 15; Ewing, Robert, farmer; 9

August 1796; to serve until 21

Matthews, Joseph; 6 April 1785; 11; Ewing, Robert; 9 August 1796; to serve until 21

Crowley, Matthew of John; 10 March 1787; 9; Hartshorn, John, farmer; 9 August 1796; to serve until 21

Pritchet, Amos of Benjamin; 20 June 1787; 9; Hartshorn, John, farmer; 9 August 1796; to serve until 21

Adams, Samuel of John. (Mary Adams, mother); 1781; 15; Evans, James, house carpenter; 15 August 1796; to serve until 21

Watt, John, son of James; 12 August 1786; 10; McGreath, William, shoemaker; 11 October 1796; to serve until 21

Hamilton, George of George (Sidney George signs indenture); 26 January 1789; 7; White, Levi, wagon maker; 12 October 1796; to serve until 21

McBride, Bendict; 14 October 1783; 13; Toland, Joshua, cordwainer; 21 November 1796; to serve until 21

Davison, John; - ; 6; Kirk, William, clothier; 6 December 1796; to serve until 21

Welsh, Jenny, daughter of William Welsh; 16 March 1790; 8; Hegan, James and Catherine; 4 February 1797; to serve until 16

Phillips, Samuel, son of Nicholas. (Lydia Coolin, mother); - ; - ; Simpson, Richard, wheelwright; 5 February 1797; to serve 6 years, 10 months

Davis, William of Elizabeth Davis; 1781; 15; Mansfield, Richard, blacksmith; 11 February 1797; to serve until 21

Husler, John of William; 1778; 18; Mansfield, Richard, blacksmith; 11 February 1797; to serve until 21

Jones, William of Jane; 1 June 1785; 11; Carr, Robert, shoemaker; 14 February 1797; to serve until 21

Lee, Elias of Ephraim; 1 February 1786; 10; Walmsley, Robert, farmer Corden; 6 March 1797; to serve until 21

Johnson, Charles, of Jacob; 25 March 1780; 17; Ash, George, shoemaker; 8 March 1797; to serve until 21

Cashner, John of Daniel; 5 June 1780; 17; Ash, George, shoemaker; 8 March 1797; to serve until 21

Johnson, Jonathan of Jacob; 11 April 1779; 18; Johnson, Charles, millwright; 8 March 1797; to serve until 21

McGarity, Ann of Richard; 30 August 1786; 10; Peden, Hugh & Elizabeth; 20 March 1797; to serve until 21

Thomas, Mary, daughter of Isaac; 29 October 1785; 11; Miller, Lewis; 11 April 1797; to serve until 21

Rutter, Thomas of Samuel; 22 November 1782; 14; Howard, William, wagon maker; 11 April 1797; to serve until 21

Jones, William; - ; - ; Wallace, Michael, miller; 11 April 1797; to serve until 21

Rutter, Moses of Samuel; 30 November 1784; 12; Pennington, William Canby, sadler; 12 April 1797; to serve until 21

Hedham, John of Henry; 13 October 1782; 14; Briscoe, Tobias & Samuel, millers; 12 April 1797; to serve until 21

Allen, Thomas; December 1878; 19; Allen, John, waterman; 12 April 1797; to serve 1 year, 8 months, 19 days

Shurmizer, Jacob, son of John; 27 April 1781; 16; Smith,

Henry, shoemaker; 13 June
1797; -
Pennington, Sarah; March,
1793; 4; Brown, Samuel; 13
June 1797; to serve until
age 16
Scrivan, George of George; 21
May 1781; 16; Evans,
Samuel, farmer; 14 June
1797; to serve until 21
Tolbum, Deborah; February
1786; 11; England, Elisha;
17 June 1797; to serve until
16
Lynch, William, son of
William; 1785; 12; Hill,
George, blacksmith; 9
August 1797; to serve until
21
Stedham, Henry; 6 March
1781; 16; Pennington, John,
shoemaker; 9 August 1797;
to serve until 21
Neal, Rebeccah; 6 November
1791; 5; McGraw, William,
shoemaker; 10 October
1797; to serve until 16
Ford, Juliet, daughter of Bettey
Ford, free Negro; 6 July
1786; 11; Rogers, Thomas,
miller; 7 October 1797; to
serve until 18
Hodgson, James; 1 May 1787;
10; McCrakin, James,
planter; 10 October 1797; to
serve until 21
Beehan, William Richardson;
24 July 1781; 16;
Chambers, Richard, taylor;

30 December 1797; to serve
until 21
Bryan, Phillip; 10 September
1783; 14; Ward, John,
farmer; 13 February 1798;
to serve until 21
Crowley, Matthew of John; - ; -
; Miller, Dr. William
(transferred by Agnes
Hartshorn); 6 March 1798;
to serve until 21
Wright, Margaret; 15 June
1791; 7; McCrery, John; 12
June 1798; to serve until 21
Kirkpatrick, James of Eleanor;
16 April 1798; 16;
McBride, James,
blacksmith; 15 May 1798;
to serve 4 years, 11 months
Johnson, David of Jacob; 20
December 1781; 17;
Matthews, John, stone
mason; 12 June 1798; to
serve until 21
Gillespie, Samuel of William; -
; - ; Chandler, Francis B.,
Frederick Town, Cecil Co.
merchant; 28 May 1798; to
serve 6 years, 6 months
Negro Thom, son of Jean
Thom; 1 October 1789; 8;
Tanner, Joseph, farmer; 16
August 1798; to serve until
21
Alcorn, George; 7 November
1791; 7; Hollingsworth,
Henry, clothier; 7
September 1798; to serve
until 21

Nowland, Benedict; 24 January 1782; 16; Walmsley, William, blacksmith; 3 September 1798; to serve until 21

Money, Thomas of Eleanor; 5 December 1781; 16; Stephenson, David, blacksmith; 9 October 1798; to serve until 21

Armstrong, Mary; - ; 6; Hall, Isaac; 31 December 1799; to serve until 16

Crowley, James; December 1788; 10; Walker, John, farmer; 9 January 1799; to serve until 18

Long, Robert of Alexander (with the consent of his mother Hannah Long; October 1787; 11; Reynolds, Jonathan, farmer; 7 February 1799; to serve until 17

Long, Elizabeth of Alexander (with the consent of her mother Hannah Long; 16 December 1788; 10; Reynolds, Samuel; 13 February 1799; to serve until 16

Duncan, Hannah; 1 January 1789; 10; Jordan, John, North Milford hundred; 7 March 1799; to serve 6 years

McLaughlin, Mary (by consent of her mother, Ann Havey); 4 September 1787; 11;

Wilson, Elizabeth; 9 March 1799; to serve until 16

Galliher, Abraham; 21 December 1794; 5; Job, Daniel Jr., blacksmith; 2 May 1799; to serve until 21

Wright, David; 30 June 1791; 7; Cochran, Robert, weaver; 20 May 1799; to serve until 21

Beetle, William; 24 May 1795; 4; Gilpin, Samuel, farmer; 24 May 1799; to serve until 21

Hill, Joseph; 20 February 1796; 3; Cully, George, cooper; - ; to serve until 21

McCullogh, Andrew (With the affirmation of his brother, Alexander McCullogh; 29 May 1785; 14; Patten, Thomas, carpenter; 18 May 1799; to serve until 21

Edmondson, James; 12 January 1781; 18; Chapple, William, nail maker; 11 June 1799; to serve until 21

Edmondson, Blaney; 24 December 1782; 17; Chapple, William, nail maker; 11 June 1799; to serve until 21

Hynson, Thomas (orphan); 7 April 1786; 13; Chapple, William, nail maker; 11 June 1799; to serve until 21

Bolton, John of Joseph; 8 August 1791; 7;

Hollingsworth, Henry; 12 June 1797; to serve until 21

Smith, Richard of Michael; 25 March 1783; 16; Pritchard, Carvil, Elkton, hat maker; - ; to serve until 21

Holton, Benjamin; Last day of November 1787; 11; Severson, Hance, farmer; 5 August 1799; to serve until 21

Boyd, William; 17 March 1787; 7; Gilpin, Samuel, farmer; 14 August 1799; to serve until 21

Bantham, Benjamin; 1796; 15; Heath, Richard Key, blacksmith; 18 February 1800; to serve 5 years and 4 months

Seager, Josiah (with the consent of his mother, Catherine Rea); 26 July 1791; 8; Lowry, James; 13 March 1800; to serve until 21

Parsely, Mary; 1 July 1790; 9; Stevenson, David; 15 March1800; to serve until 16

Fox, John; 25 June 1784; 15; Hollingsworth, Henry, tanner; - ; to serve 6 years, 3 months

Patten, Sophia; 11 April 1791; 9; Preston, William; 20 April 1800; to serve until 16

Williams, Elizabeth (with the consent of her mother, Margaret Williams); 9 September 1796; 3; Brown, Elisha, West Nottingham, Cecil Co.; 21 April 1890; to serve until 16

Welch, Sarah; 14 February 1791; 9; Reynolds, Jonathan; 20 April 1800; to serve until 16

Welch, John; 3 September 1794; 5; Preston, William, farmer; 20 April 1800; to serve until 21

Whitelock, James; 15 December 1783; 16; White, Jacob, farmer; 2 April 1800; to serve until 21

Sutton, Jock; 15 January 1796; 4; Jackson, James, miller; 7 April 1800; to serve until 21

Hance, James; 7 March 1785; 15; Wallace, Samuel Patterson, cooper; 8 April 1800; to serve until 21

Hynson, Thomas; 7 April 1786; 14; Hollingsworth, Henry, weaver; 9 April 1800; to serve until 21

Edmundson, Blany; 24 December 1789; 18; Atkin, John, clothier; 9 April 1800; to serve until 21

Greenland, Abner, Lancaster Co.; 7 July 1783; 16; Haines, Eli, clothier; 9 April 1800; to serve until 21

Willson, Margaret of William; 13 September 1786; 13;

Partridge, James; 10 June 1800; to serve until 16

Willson, Mary of William; 29 January 1798; 11; Lecky, Thomas; 10 June 1800; to serve until 16

Ward, Samuel, son of Thomas; 30 October 1789; 10; Bravard, Joshua, farmer; 11 June 1800; to serve until 21

Hill, James; December 1782; 18; Beard, George, farmer; 26 June 1800; to serve until 21

Hopkins, John (With the consent of his parents); 1787; 12; Reynolds, Samuel, farmer; 27 June 1800; to serve until 21

Hopkins, Joseph; 1789; 11; Haines, Reuben, farmer; 27 June 1800; to serve until 21

Green, Edward; 25 December 1789; 10; Moore, Joseph, farmer; 14 July 1800; to serve until 21

Alexander, Ephraim; 14 August 1790; 10; Hall, John; 1 August 1800; to serve until 21

McCoy, Joseph; November 1789; 10; McCoy, Alexander, cooper; 5 August 1800; to serve until 21

Thompson, Mary, daughter of William; 2 June 1790; 10; Rogers, Catherine; 12

August 1800; to serve until 16

Baker, James Thompson, son of James; 23 December 1788; 11; Miller, Lewis; 13 August 1800; to serve until 21

Barnett, Thomas of Joshua; 1 October 1784; 16; McCarlin, Robert, manufacturer of flour; 14 October 1800; to serve until 21

Buckram, James (A Negro boy, son of Mary Buckram; 23 February 1887; 13; Sweany, David, farmer; 15 October 1800; to serve until 21

Beaston, George Hughes; 5 March 1784; 16; Beaston, Zebulon, hatter; 10 December 1800; to serve until 21

Price, John N.; 23 February 1791; 9; Beaston, Zebulon, hatter; 10 December 1800; to serve until 21

Whittaker, William, son of Ralph; 6 March 1784; 16; Wilkinson, Robert, Cartwright & blacksmith; 24 December 1800; to serve until 21

Conner, James Chadick; 11 September 1783; 17; Howard, William, Blacksmith; - ; to serve until 21

Burgoyne, John; 2 January 1784; 16; Johnson, Charles, millwright; 11 April 1800; to serve until 21

Burgoyne, Margaret; 3 January 1789; 11; Slicer, John, sawyer; 14 April 1801; to serve until 16

Jemmar, Patrick Henry; 2 August 1786; 14; Hall, James, blacksmith; 14 April 1801; to serve until 21

Bell, John, of William; 16 March 1791; 10; Ratliff, James, farmer; 14 April 1801; to serve until 21

Ninian, a Negro boy; 12 July 1800; 1; Taylor, Thomas, farmer; 15 April 1801; to serve until 21

Ewing, John of Alexander; 1784; 17; Patten, Thomas, Carpenter; 21 May 1801; to serve until 21

McCoy, John; 16 March 1784; 17; Rogers, Thomas, miller; 11 May 1801; to serve until 21

Biddle, John; 17 January 1797; 3; Leech, William, cooper; 8 June 1801; to serve until 21

Davison, Robert; 23 October 1783; 17; Ramsey, James, shoemaker; 9 June 1801; to serve until 21

Young, William of Robert; 1 February 1791; 10; Gilleland, Thomas, saddler; 8 August 1801; to serve until 21

Welch, Robert, with the consent of his mother Elizabeth Welch; 25 April 1796; 5; Moore, William, miller; 10 August 1801; to serve until 21

Hugg, Richard of William; 20 June 1784; 17; Shattach, Levi, shoemaker; 11 August 1801; to serve until 21

Smith, Delia, daughter of Hannah Smith, Negro; 2 January 1792; 9; Robinson, Henry; 11 August 1801; to serve until 16

Lemmon, Archibald, son of Archibald; 22 January 1794; 7; George, Sidney, farmer; 11 August 1801; to serve until 21

Dunlap, Lucretia; 24 January 1790; 11; Mifflin, John; 1 September 1801; to serve until 16

Ross, John; 18 November 1897; 3; Reynolds, Jonathan, farmer; 9 September 1801; to serve until 21

Cunningham, John; 5 October 1794; 2; Coulson, Abner, joiner; 5 October 1801; to serve until 21

Lowe, John, son of John; 9 May 1796; 11; Alexander, Justice, cooper; 13 October 1801; to serve until 21

Hodgson, James; 1 May 1787; 14; McCrakin, John, cooper; 13 October 1801; to serve until 21

Bennett, Eli; 17 January 1789; 12; Moore, Alexander, blacksmith; 13 October 1801; to serve until 21

Wilson, Levina, daughter of William; 7 January 1795; 6; Partridge, James; 14 October 1801; to serve until 16

Callinden, John; 14 October 1785; 16; Beaston, Zebulon, hatter; 14 October 1801; to serve until 21

Leech, Robert of John; 25 May 1776; 18; Tylon, Isaac, hatter; 14 October 1801; to serve until 21

McVey, Benjamin, son of Mary Bing; 7 November 1788; 13; Bing, John, cooper; 8 December 1801; to serve until 21

Reese, Matilda, daughter of Lucretia McKinley; 22 November 1786; 5; Kean, John; 8 December 1801; to serve until 16

Thompson, William of William; 8 April 1786; 15; Kean, John, taylor; 8 December 1801; to serve until 21

Adams, John; 4 April 1787; 14; Rowls, Elihu, taylor; 8

December 1801; to serve until 21

Murphy, Margaret; 20 May 1792; 12; Springer, Mary Ann; - ; to serve until 16

Tweedy, James, with the consent of his mother, Susannah Tweedy; 27 March 1784; 17; Pennington, Joseph, wheelwright; 30 January 1802; to serve until 21

Carl/Corl, Mary; 4 September 1796; 5; Jones, James; 9 February 1802; to serve until 16

Dickson, Andrew; 25 December 1796; 5; Taggert, Peter, weaver; 9 February 1802; to serve until 21

Kuisler, William, son of William; 25 March 1797; 15; Tyson, Levi, miller; 9 February 1802; to serve until 21

Perry, Israel, with the consent of his mother; 1 March 1794; 8; Reynolds, Richard, farmer; 8 March 1802; to serve until 21

Caldwell, Thomas, with the consent of his parents, Thomas & Katherine Caldw; - ; 11; Haines, Thomas, farmer; 3 May 1802; to serve until 17

McElwee, Samuel of John; 29 November 1789; 12;

Haines, Eli, potter; 3 May 1802; to serve until 21
Browne, Edmund of Arrowsmith & Mary; 20 April 1787; 14; Miller, Lewis, house carpenter; 17 May 1802; to serve until 21
Springer, Peter of Joseph; 20 May 1784; 18; Howard, William, wheelwright; 8 June 1802; to serve until 21
Tweedy, David, son of David; 15 June 1778; 12; Howard, William, wheelwright; 8 June 1802; to serve until 21
Allcock, Thomas, of William; 19 March 1778; 12; Smith, Henry, shoemaker; 9 June 1802; to serve until 21
Rutter, Moses of Samuel; 30 November 1797; 17; Rickets, George, sadler; 9 June 1802; to serve until 21
Holmes, George, son of William (with the consent of his father; 12 January 1781; 11; Hollingsworth, John, Stafford County, Va.; miller; 13 June 1802; to serve until 21
Bolleson, Charles (with the consent of his mother); 12 February 1786; 16; Pearce, William, carpenter; 4 August 1802; to serve until 21
Calwell, John of Thomas; 6 March 1793; 9; Taylor,

Noble, shoemaker; 6 August 1802; to serve until 21
Ware, William of Thomas (with the consent of his father); 4 August 1791; 11; Ratliff, James, farmer; 10 August 1802; 10 August 1802
Jarrett, Elisha of Sarah (Negro); 1 August 1801; 1; Taylor, Thomas, farmer; 10 August 1802; to serve until 21
Kelly, Thomas (son of Mary Dixon); 1 January 1792; 10; Maxwell, James, farmer; 11 August 1802; to serve until 21
Burris, James (with the consent of his guardian, Thomas McMullen); 14 April 1785; 17; Patton, John, chairmaker; 20 November 1802; to serve until 21
Roney, Sarah (an illigitimate child); not given; about 10; Ewing, Putnam; 15 December 1802; to serve until 16
Negro Abraham (with the consent of Hannah Orrick, admin. for James Orrick; 19 October 1793; 12; White, Thomas; 5 March 1803.; to serve until 21, then free
McMillun, John (with the consent of his father Robert McMullin; not given; 13; Coulson, George, tanner; 9

March 1803; to serve until 21

Brackley, John, son of Andrew; 7 April 1802; 9; McCullogh, John, cabinetmaker; 9 March 1803; to serve until 21

Connor, Elinor; 18 July 1799; 4; Condon, Samuel; - ; to serve until 16

Kidman, Mary, daughter of Jane Erwin/Ervin; 27 February 1789; 14; Miller, Samuel; 20 March 1803; to serve until 16

Long, John; 18 April 1801; 2; Porter, John, carpenter; 12 March 1803; to serve until 21

Campbell, Letitia of John (with the consent of her mother, Ann Campbell); 1789; 13; Rodgers, Rowland; 22 March 1803; to serve until 16

Price, Joshua; 15 December 1793; 9; Wickes, James, blacksmith; 4 April 1803; to serve until 21

Caruthers, George; May 1789; 14; Gay, Samuel, blacksmith; 12 April 1803; to serve until 21

Ralston, Joseph of Jesse; 15 January 1792; 11; McCaslin, Robert, miller; 13 April 1803; to serve until 21

Broom, Richard; 10 August 1799; 3; Stevenson, John, farmer; 15 April 1803; to serve until 21

Gibson, Elizabeth; 20 December 1792; 10; Rogers, Thomas; 23 May 1803; to serve until 16

Willson, Levina; 17 January 1795; 8; Coudon, Rachel; 14 June 1803; to serve until 16

Sullivan, William; 6 April 1789; 14; Brown, Elisha, cooper; 14 June 1803; to serve until 21

Crookshanks, William; not given; 7; McDowell, William; - ; to serve until 21

Crookshanks, John; not given; 13; Carswell, John, weaver; 14 June 1803; to serve until 21

Willson, William; 15 June 1788; 15; Smith, David, scrivener; 15 June 1803; to serve until 21

Graish, Edward of Edward; 3 April 1788; 15; Graham, William, carpenter; 30 June 1803; to serve until 21

McCardle, James, (with the consent of his father John McCardle; 22 May 1797; 6; Cameron, John Sr., farmer; 21 July 1803; to serve until 21

Bulltell, Henry Empson; 1 December 1784; 18;

Dennis, John, shoemaker; 9 August 1803; to serve until 21

Bell, Mary; 1 February 1793; 10; Bryan, John; 9 August 1803; to serve until 16

Bailey, John; 10 February 1789; 14; Brown, Robert, cart wright and wagon maker; 9 August 1803; to serve until 21

Beech, Mary; 26 December 1800; 3; Hall, James; 20 September 1803; to serve until 16

Negro Thom; 1799; 14; Schiltree, Matthews, farmer; 11 October 1803; to serve until 21

Crookshanks, Nancy (with the consent of her mother); 28 March 1793; 10; Cummings, David; 7 October 1803; to serve until 16

Longwell, Robert, son of Robert Longwell, North Millford Hundred; August 1785; 18; Sample, John, Carpenter; 6 December 1803; to serve 2 years, 7 months from this date

Murphy, Stephen; 15 September 1784; 9; Crookshanks, John, carpenter; 16 December 1803; to serve until 21

White, John (with the consent of his parents, William and Katherine White); - ; - ; Walsh, William, hammerman; 7 April 1804; to serve 3 years from the 6 February 1803

Hindman, Mary; 1 April 1793; 9; Ewing, Henry; 2 April 1804; to serve until 16

Hynson, Thomas; 7 April 1755; 18; Hollingsworth, William, tanner; 11 April 1804; to serve until 21

Bryson, Thomas, son of Thomas; 1 February 1789; 15; Foard, John H., tanner; 10 April 1804; to serve until 21

White, Abner; 28 April 1789; 15; Hughes, Joseph, blacksmith; 7 May 1804; to serve until 21

Hanna, Richard, son of Mary Cobourn; 24 July 1787; 17; Reynolds, Stephen; 28 May 1804; to serve until 21

French, James Ross, son of James; 12 June 1795; 9; Harlan, Joseph, miller; 12 June 1804; to serve until 21

Jordan, William, son of Jane being a poor black child; 10 September 1782; 12; Donald, James B., farmer; 12 June 1804.; to serve until 21

Cosby, Fatima; 14 June 1796; 8; Moore, George; 11 August 1804; to serve until 16

French, Samuel; 3 July 1794; 10; Barns, George, bootmaker; 14 August 1804; to serve until 21

Thompson, John; 21 August 1799; 15; Pricer, John Hyland, shoe & boot maker; 14 August 1804; to serve until 21

Shaffer, James; 29 January 1800; 4; Taylor, Robert, plasterer; 14 August 1804; to serve until 21

Phillips, Zebulon; 3 August 1797; 13; Huslar, John, blacksmith; 21 July 1804; to serve until 21

Williams, Thomas, son of Basil; 3 March 1788; 16; Miller, Lewis, house carpenter & joiner; 16 June 1804; to serve until 21

Lackland, Samuel; 26 July 1788; 16; Brown, David, blacksmith; 18 August 1804; to serve until 21

Charles, a Mulatto; 30 November 1799; 4; Jones, James, farmer; 1 January 1805; to serve until 21

Thrieth, James; April, 1782; 12; Courad, John, tanner & carrier; 8 January 1805; to serve until 21

Willson, Darcus; 17 March 1787; 13; Barns, George; 8 January 1805; to serve until 16

Wimble, John of John; 2 November 1787; 17; Ginn, John, blacksmith; 15 January 1805; to serve until 21

Hukin, Elijah; 23 September 1788; 16; Cowan, William; 12 February 1805; to serve until 21

Rutter, Margary; 13 January 1782; 12; Price, John H.; 12 February 1805; to serve until 16

Killpatrick, John, son of Nancy Boyer; 13 January 1892; 15; Chambers, Nicholas, farmer; 6 March 1805; to serve until 21

Davis, William, son of William; 15 April 1801; - ; Jordan, John, farmer; 12 March 1805; to serve until 21

Handshaw, Amos; 23 January 1897; 8; Reynolds, John, blacksmith; 3 April 1805; to serve until 21

Benington, Jean; - ; 5; Moore, William C; 8 April 1805; to serve until 16

Morrison, Rebeccah; - ; 4; Bell, Richard; 8 April 1805; to serve until 16

Reeves, Robert; 17 July 1792; 12; Gatchel, Elisha; 8 April 1805; to serve until 21

Jackson, John; 3 September 1789; 15; Patten, Thomas,

carpenter; 9 April 1805; to serve until 21

Pugh, James; 25 November 1800; 5; Bravard, Joshua, farmer; 26 April 1805; to serve until 21

Moody, Isaac, of Alexander; 6 November 1790; 15; Price, John H., shoemaker; 30 May 1805; to serve until 21

Moody, David of Alexander; 16 November 1792; 12; Price, John H., shoemaker; 30 May 1805; to serve until 21

Dick, Samuel; 1 February 1789; 16; Howard, Thomas, blacksmith; 2 May 1805; to serve until 21

Quail, Elizabeth; 7 October 1793; 11; Ratliff, James; 11 June 1805; to serve until 16

Humes, Agnes, daughter of William Hume; 15 February 1798; 15; Johnston, George; 15 June 1805; to serve until 16

Mackey, William Beard, by consent of his mother, Anne Lewis; 3 October 1788; 16; Conrad, John; 21 June 1805; to serve until 21

Porper, James, an orphan black child; 25 February 1781; 14; Allen, Rebecca; 20 July 1805; to serve until 21

Pritchard, James; 25 March 1780; 15; Rutter, Thomas,

blacksmith; 13 August 1805; to serve until 21

Yeoman, John, with the consent of his mother, Elizabeth Yeoman; 10 October 1782; 13; Patten, John, chairmaker & turner; 11 October 1805; to serve until 21

Ball, Ezekill, with the consent of his mother, Susannah Murran; 7 May 1786; 9; Gay, Samuel Jr., blacksmith; 16 December 1805; to serve until 21

Crow, Owen, son of Owen; 31 May 1789; 16; Beaston, Zebulon, hatter; 27 November 1805; to serve until 21

Galloway, Robert, son of John Galloway; 15 May 1789; 16; Husler, John, blacksmith; 10 December 1805; to serve until 21

Crouch, Sarah, daughter of Edward Crouch; 10 December 1797; 9; Holt, Joseph; 16 January 1806; to serve until 16

Crouch, Susanah; 24 March 1795; 12; Holt, Jesse; 16 June 1805; to serve until 16

Pugh, Joseph of James; 30 November 1786; 20; Wallace, James, tanner; 25 January 1806; to serve until 21 (30 November 1817)

Williams, Jesse, with the consent of his mother; 2 October 1788; 18; Oldham, Nathanial, blacksmith & wagon maker; 31 December 1805; to serve until 21

Sheppard, David, with the consent of his mother; 14 February 1797; 8; Oldham, Nathanial, blacksmith & wagon maker; 2 December 1805; to serve until 21

Tony, Millie, a free black girl; 11 August 1793; 12; Louttit, Henry, a free black man; 23 December 1805; to serve until 16

Taylor, Joseph; 21 December 1794; 12; Beaston, Zebulon, hatter; 12 February 1806; to serve until 21

Burk, Nathanial; 1 November 1789; 16; Bryan, John, farmer; 12 February 1806; to serve until 21

Matthews, Jane, daughter of Robert Matthews; 11 November 1798; 7; Massitt/Maffitt, Samuel; 17 September 1805; to serve until 16

Long, John; February 1783; 13; Logun, Thomas, cooper; 20 December 1806; to serve until 21

Neal, John of John; 1787; 19; McCorkle, James A., carpenter; 9 April 1806; to serve 2 years, 7 months, until 21

Neal, Joseph of John; - ; - ; McCorkle, James A., carpenter; 9 April 1806; to serve 8 years

Willcocks, William of William; 15 November1790; 13; Wilkinson, Robert, wheelwright; 23 April 1806; to serve until 21

Armour, John, son of Hugh; 1 June 1791; 15; McDowell, Samuel, cooper; 16 June 1806; 16 June 1806; to serve until 21

Alexander, Ephraim, an illegitimate boy; 17 August 1789; 16; Hall, Richard, blacksmith; 6 June 1806.; to serve until 21

Kennedy, John with consent of Moses Kennedy, (Father?); 1795; 9; Barns, George; 20 June 1806; to serve until 21

Adcock, Thomas; 12 March 1790; 16; Kassner, David; - ; to serve until 21

Jackson, John, son of Molly Ke__ihan/Kertikart; 3 September 1789; 16; Patter, John, chain striker & tinner; - ; to serve until 21

Patterson, William; - ; 17; Patten, Thomas, carpenter; - ; to serve until 21

Merryman, John, with the consent of his uncle Joseph Smith, a black man. His mother, Jane Patterson being removed from the state; 22 February 1787; 9; Chandlee, James, farmer; 15 July 1806; to serve until 21

Regen, Rachel by James Regen, Chester Co. Pennsylvania (her father); 24 November 1786; 7; Reynolds, Jonathan and Elizabeth; 1 October 1806; to serve until 16

McKeaver, Thomas by Charles M. McKeaver, His father; - ; - ; Alexander, Alexander, blacksmith; 31 January 1807; to serve until 12 November 1812

Long, John; 1 October 1792; 13; Hall, Richard, blacksmith; 22 February 1806; to serve until 21

Lowry, Rebeccah, with the consent of Fannie Thomas Anderson, her mother; 12 September 1800; 7; Standish, Miles; 13 January 1807; to serve until 16

McKever, Alexander; 1 January 1797; 10; Christe, Robert, stone mason; 5 February 1807; to serve until 5 January 1818

Kirkill, John, son of Joseph; 13 June 1781; 15; McCracken, John, blacksmith; 10 February 1807; to serve until 21

Davison, John; 21 July 1780; 16; Kartner, Daniel, shoe and boot maker; 10 February 1807; to serve until 21

Williams, Elizabeth of Basil; 11 August 1796; 8; Haines, Job Jr.; 10 February 1807; to serve until 16

Thompson, Robert, with the consent of his mother, Catherine Price; 25 January 1795; 12; Kesler, John, blacksmith; 14 March 1807; to serve until 25 January 1816

McCoy, John H.; 19 April 1793; 14; Miller, Lewis, carpenter; 8 April 1807; to serve until 21

Armstrong, Andrew of Cornelius; 25 January 1781; 16; Howard, Thomas, blacksmith; 16 April 1807; to serve until 21

Rabb, John of Anthony; 8 June 1779; 18; Howard, Thomas, blacksmith; 16 April 1807; to serve until 21

McDowell, Eavan, with consent of his father, Thomas McDowell; 6 April 1798; 12; Paxson, Charles; 23 May 1807; to serve until 6 April 1815

McDowell, Nancy, with consent of her father, Thomas McDowell; 17 May 1800; 7; Paxson, Charles and Anne; 23 May 1807; to serve until 6 April 1815

Work, William, with the consent of his father, Samuel Work; 9 September 1789; 17; Howard, William, wheelwright and blacksmith; 25 July 1807; to serve until 21

Rickets, John of John (cooper); 10 June 1789; 18; Howard, William, wheelwright and blacksmith; 25 July 1807; to serve until 21

Dolan, Thomas; 26 August 1792; 14; Wilkinson, Robert, cartwright & blacksmith; 8 August 1807; to serve until 21

Meekins, Richard, with the consent of his mother Susannah Sipples & his stepfather Henry Sipples; - ; 14; Reed, Charles, boatmaker; 1 August 1807; to serve until 21

Lueens, Mary (with the consent of her mother, Mary Lueens; 2 October 1793; 13; Moore, Eloner; 6 August 1807; to serve until 16

Quin, George (with the consent of his father John Quin); 1 September 1794; 12; Smith, David; 10 August 1807; to serve util age 16

Hall, Lewis Gray, with the consent of his stepmother; - ; - ; Patten, Thomas,

carpenter; - ; to serve until 21

Hargen, Eli; 13 October 1794; 16; Cameron, John, blacksmith; 13 October 1807; to serve until 21

Wood, Thomas, with the consent of his father Samuel Wood; 17 September 1795; 12; Rogers, Thomas, farmer; 17 November 1807; to serve until 21

McVey, Joshua Davis, an illegitimate child; 26 April 1795; 12; Magraw, James, farmer; 5 November 1807; to serve until 17

Black, Margaret of Joseph; - ; 5; Magraw, James; 5 November 1807; to serve 10 years and eight months

Black, Robert of Joseph; - ; - ; Magraw, James; 5 November 1807; to serve 11 years, 8 months

Gorrell, Archibald; 1798; 10; White, Thomas, farmer; 29 February 1808; to serve until age 16

Kinkead, William; 8 September 1792; 16; Howard, Thomas, blacksmith & wheelwright; 1 March 1808; to serve until age 21

Hartshorn, Thomas, with the consent of his mother, Nancy Hartshorn; 6 August 1798; 9; Ramsey, Samuel, farmer; 4 April 1808; to serve until age 17

Ritchie, Jesse, son of James; 24 May 1791; 16; Beaston, Zebulon, hatter; 12 April 1808; to serve until age 21

Nisbett, Joseph Gordon, with the consent of his father, Alexander Nisbitt; 1791; 17; Patton, Thomas, carpenter; 21 March 1808; to serve until age 21

Morgan, Thomas of David; 1789; 18; Robert John, cabinet maker, Elkton; 19 December 1807; to serve for three years

Irwin, Jesse, son of John; 1801; 7; Irwin, Abner, North Milford, weaver; 8 June 1808; to serve until age 21

Pennington, John; 4 November 1791; 16; Robert John, cabinet maker, Elkton; 4 June 1808; to serve until age 21

Owings, Rachael, with consent of her mother, Ruth Owings; 1 November 1807; 10; Jones, Edward J.; 30 April 1808; to serve until age 16

Knight, John, with the consent of his mother; 16 December 1797; 10; Reynolds, Stephen, miller; 7 June 1808; to serve until age 21

Rice, George, son of Sarah Moore; 10 May 1798; 10;

Ricketts, William, farmer; 14 June 1808; to serve until age 21

Kennedy, George; 10 January 1798; 10; Reynolds, Benjamin, carpenter; 16 June 1808; to serve until age 21

Realy, Isaac, son of William; 2 October 1797; 10; McKraken, John, blacksmith; 14 June 1808; to serve until age 21

Julianna, female Negress; 1 December 1801; 6; Moore, Moses; 18 June 1808; to serve until age 16

Dickey, Jane; 1 October 1804; 3; Cummings, James; 24 June 1808; to serve until age 16

Garrett, Thomas Jr., with the consent of his mother, Sarah Garrett; - ; - ; Garrett, Thomas, blacksmith; 16 May 1808; to serve for a term of 4 years

Sullivan, Aaron, with the consent of his mother, Elizabeth Sullivan; - ; - ; Garrett, Thomas, blacksmith; 3 July 1808; to serve for a term of 8 years, 3 months

Crothers, John, with the consent of Dr. James Beard, a distant relative; 8 March 1790; 16; Conrad, John, tanner; 30 March 1808; to serve until age 21

Cummings, Samuel; - ; - ; Pond, Lambert; - ; to serve until age 21

Clayton, Andrew John; 1 August 1790; 18; Booth, John; 10 August 1808; to serve until age 21

Anderson, Mary, Negro; 4 March 1804; 4; Dickson, James; 9 September 1808; to serve until age 16

Lowrey, Rebecca, with the consent of her mother Fanny Thomas Anderson; 10 November 1799; 8; Gibbons, John; 19 September 1808; to serve until age 16

Hughes, James, with the consent of his father, Edward Hughes, saddler; - ; - ; Bryan, John; - ; to serve a term of 11 years, 11 months

Haner, Hyland son of Elizabeth; 1 September 1803; 5; Edmundson, Caleb, farmer; 13 December 1808; to serve until age 21

Gibbony, Ann with the consent of her mother, Ann Gibbony; 9 July 1801; 7; Christie, James; 7 December 1808; to serve until age 16

Grant, David, with the consent of his mother, a free black woman, unnamed; 25

March 1801; 8; Cather, Hannah, accountant; 17 January 1809; to serve until age 21

Thompson, Robert, son of Robert; 6 January 1795; 14; Scott, James, cartwright; 14 February 1809; to serve until age 21

Powley, Thomas, son of John; 5 July 1794; 14; Patten, Thomas, house carpenter and joiner; 14 February 1809; to serve until age 21

Plymouth, Ben, son of Susan, 'a black woman'; 14 February 1802; 7; Moore, Alexander, farmer; 14 February 1809; to serve until age 21

Dunken, Samuel; 15 February 1802; 7; Phillips, Joseph, bootmaker; 15 February 1809; to serve until age 21

Price, John N, son of Ann Price; 23 February 1790; 18; Scott, Moses, blacksmith; 15 February 1809; to serve until age 21

Price, Thomas, son of Nancy Phillips; 11 January 1796; 13; Scott, Thomas, house carpenter; 15 February 1809; to serve until age 21

Taylor, John, son of Luke; 17 November 1781; 17; Evans, William, blacksmith; 11 March 1809; to serve until age 21

Laird, Miller, with the consent of his mother; 16 February 1793; 17; Cumings, James, stocking maker; 5 April 1809; to serve until age 21

Winchester, Timothy, with the consent of his mother ___ Winchester; 11 February 1793; 17; Cumings, James, stocking maker; 5 April 1809; to serve until age 21

Smith, Steward; - ; 7; Preston, William; 6 April 1809; to serve until age 21

Ryland, Sussanah, illegitimate child; 9 December 1801; 7; Reynolds, Thomas; 7 April 1809; to serve until age 16

Connaly, Charles; - ; - ; Scott, Thomas, carpenter; 6 April 1809; to serve for a term of five years, four months

Dalrymple, James; 2 March 1794; 15; McCraekin, John, blacksmith; 11 April 1809; to serve until age 21

Beck, Obediah; 10 May 1792; 17; Undergroves, Richard, blacksmith; 11 April 1809; to serve until age 21

Cashore, William; 9 October 1794; 13; McDowell, Robert, weaver; 12 April 1809; to serve until age 21

Hodgson, James; 10 May 1791; 17; Crachen, James, blacksmith; 11 April 1809; to serve until age 21

Hannah, Joseph, with the consent of his father, Joseph Hannah; 2 October 1798; 10; Cully, George Jr., cooper; 2 January 1808; to serve until age 21

Hannah, Samuel, with the consent of his father, Joseph Hannah; 3 October 1800; 8; McCully, John, cooper; 10 February 1808; to serve until age 21

Crothers, William, son of William, late of Cecil County, James Beard, guardian; 1 May 1793; 15; See, Peter, tailor; 21 April 1809; to serve until 1 May 1814 (age 21)

Buckram, Joseph, with the consent of his mother Moly Buckram, a black woman; 14 November 1800; 7; Churchman, George Jr., farmer; 21 April 1809; to serve until age 21

Jenkins, Rachel, a black illegitimate child; - ; - ; Henderson, David; 22 April 1809; to serve until age 16

William, A black boy; 21 April 1803; 6; York, Benjamin, farmer; 22 April 1809; to serve until age 21

Leonard, Mary; 3 July 1799; 9; Gatchell, Elisha; 13 May 1809; to serve until age 16

Veazey, Benoni; 26 October 1793; 15; Kirk, John, boot

maker; 19 June 1809; to serve until age 21

Ringler, John, son of Jonathan; 1 September 1808; 9; Degrove, Richard, farmer; 14 June 1809; to serve until age 21

Cato, Josiah, Negro; 25 June 1794; 14; Rogers, William; 10 June 1809; to serve until age 21

Cox, Noble; 17 February 1797; 12; Rogers, William; 10 June 1809; to serve until age 21

Julianna; 21 December 1802; 7; Brown, William; 19 June 1809; to serve until age 16

Ruley, James Henry; 2 January 1804; 5; Reynolds, William, farmer; 13 June 1809; to serve until age 21

Fulton, James; 2 May 1803; 6; Laws/Lows, Robert, farming; 15 June 1809; to serve until age 21

Branson, James G; 1794; 15; Brown, Caleb, cartwright; 176 June 1809; to serve until age 21

Brown, David, with the consent of his mother, a free black woman; 25 October 1796; 12; Dunbar, Andrew, farmer; 14 June 1809; to serve until age 21

Irwin, James; 1 March 1804; 5; Blackburn, Uriah,

blacksmith; 16 September 1809; to serve until age 21

Jacob, a Black Boy; May 1800; 9; Hyland, John of Jacob, farmer; 27 September 1809; to serve until age 21

Leonard, John; 1 June 1801; 8; Armstrong, William, farmer; 6 November 1809; to serve until 17

Sullivan, Nathan; 30 October 1797; 12; Garrett, William, miller; 12 December 1809; to serve until age 21

Crawford, William; not given; not given; Cowan, William, merchant; 29 December 1809; to serve until 15 January 1818

Brackley, John; 17 April 1793; 16; McGowen, John, shoemaker; 2 January 1810; to serve until age 21

Marshall, James, with the consent of Hugh Beard, guardian; 15 January 1810; - ; Brown, Robert Jr., blacksmith; 15 January 1810; to serve until 22 May 1814

Bryrgoyne, Richard, son of James; 15 September 1793; 16; Karshner, Daniel, boot maker; 13 February 1810; to serve until age 21

Lockwood, George; 17 November 1797; 12; Blackburn, Samuel,

blacksmith; 4 January 1810; to serve until age 21

Robb, Levi, son of Anthony; 2 April 1799; 11; Devlin, John, weaver; 22 March 1810; to serve until age 21

Bacon, Susannah, with the consent of her father, a man of color; 25 July 1796; 13; Reynolds, Jacob, farmer; 31 March 1810; to serve until age 16

Cummins, James; 31 March 1810; - ; Wallaston, Joseph, cartwright and blacksmith; 3 April 1810; to serve until age 21

Knight, Azor; 4 June 1793; 17; Hains, Eli, potter; 4 April 1810; to serve until age 21

Porter, John; 15 November 1804; 5; Cummings, David, farmer; 16 March 1810; to serve until age 21

Golden, Jonathan; 25 March 1800; 10; Clement, Thomas, farmer; 10 April 1810; to serve until age 21

Leonard, Elizabeth; 22 November 1796; 13; Clement, Thomas, farmer; 10 April 1810; to serve until age 16

Kidd, Charles of John; 9 October 1796; 13; Alexander, Alexander, cartwright; 10 April 1810; to serve until age 21

Ferrill, James; 1 January 1799; 11; Parquet, Marcellus William, merchant & farmer; 11 April 1810; to serve until age 21

Elliott, Benjamin, son of Henry Elliott; 20 March 1802; 8; Reynolds, Thomas, farmer; 4 April 1810; to serve until 17

Elliott, Jesse, son of Henry Elliott; 20 July 1804; 6; Reynolds, Thomas; 2 April 1810; to serve until 17

Price, John N.; 23 February 1791; 19; Peery, William, cartwright and blacksmith; 4 June 1810; to serve until age 21

Wimble, Joseph; 16 July 1793; 16; Conary, Matthew, bricklayer; 13 June 1810; to serve until age 21

Catherine, daughter of Phillis, Negro; - ; - ; Hull, Ann M.; 25 May 1810; to serve for 9 years from this date, then free and manumitted

Dolan, James, son of Thomas Dolan; 2 November 1798; 11; Pearce, Benjamin, carpenter; 13 August 1810; to serve until 21

Boyd, Hugh of John; - ; - ; Gay, Samuel Jr., blacksmith; 18 August 1810; to serve for a term of 4 years from this date

Blake, John, a Negro Boy;
1805; 5; Barnett, John,
waterman; 30 August 1810;
to serve until 21

Walker, John; 1 April 1806; 4;
Fulton, Thomas, farmer; 7
September 1810; to serve
until 21

Barr, Abraham alias Wright; 1
December 1793; 17;
Reynolds, Henry, miller; 9
October 1810; to serve until
21

Negro Sarah; - ; - ; Evan W.
Thomas; 13 June 1810; to
serve a term of 12 years
from this date, then free

Negro Phillis; - ; - ; Evan W.
Thomas; 29 November
1810; to serve a term of 12
years from this date, then
free

Reynolds, Joshua; 27 February
1796; 14; Scott, Moses,
cartwright and blacksmith;
25 September 1810; to serve
until 21

Chreate, Samuel, son of John;
19 February 1796; 15;
Evans, William, blacksmith;
26 January 1811; to serve
until 21

Taylor, Samuel of Luke; 28
February 1795; 16; Dean,
John, blacksmith; 26
January 1811; to serve until
21

Lewis, Robert; 17 April 1794;
17; Bayard, Stephen,

farmer; 11 February 1811;
to serve until 21

Fergerson, Jesse, son of
Zebulon of Elkton; 4 March
1796; 15; Garrett, Thomas,
blacksmith; 29 January
1811; to serve until 21

Holliday, James, son of John; 3
February 1803; 8; Wood,
John, nail maker; 1 April
1811; to serve until 21

George, a black boy; 1 June
1798; 12; Alderidge,
Samuel; 3 April 1811; to
serve until 21

Rose, a black girl; April 1802;
9; Alderidge, Samuel; 3
April 1811; to serve until 16

Garrettt, Samuel, son of
William; 9 July 1793; 17;
Reynolds, Benjamin, house
carpenter and joiner; 9 April
1811; to serve until 21

Negro Tom, formerly the
property of Andrew Barrett,
now manumitted; - ; - ;
Patten, Thomas; 9 April
1811; to serve for 5 years
from this date, then free

Biddle, Jackson; 13 May 1803;
8; England, Isaac, farmer;
10 April 1811; to serve until
16

Todd, Levi, son of William; 11
June 1801; 9; Fulton,
William, fuller; 20 May
1811; to serve until 21

Todd, Margaret, daughter of
William; 1 March 1800; 11;

Cochran, Robert; 1 June 1811; to serve until 16 Eli, Cameron, son of James; 18 July 1803; 8; Harlan, Joseph, farmer; 11 June 1811; to serve until 17 Gillespie, Jane; 1 January 1800; 11; Ramsey, Samuel; 18 June 1811; to serve until 16

Marshall, Isaac L.; 22 March 1794; 17; Askew, Peter, tanner; 25 June 1811; to serve until 21

Carter, James, with the consent of Samuel Carter, guardian; 29 May 1795; 16; Haines, Eli, potter; 7 August 1811; to serve until 21

Brookes, John of John; 3 December 1796; 15; Howard, Thomas, wheelwright and blacksmith; 7 August 1811; to serve until 21

Richardson, Thomas; 28 December 1797; 13; John, Robert, cabinet maker; 5 September 1811; to serve until 21

McQue, Mary, daughter of Dominick; 16 January 1806; 5; Gerry, James; 5 September 1811; to serve until 16

Negro James, son of Margaret Anderson; 1 November 1804; 6; Hull, John; 9 October 1811; to serve until 21

Bates, John, son of Hamilton; - ; - ; Wilson, John, wool manufacturer; 7 November 1811; to serve until 23 May 1818

Price, Elizabeth, daughter of Veazey Price; 2 November 1798; 13; Oldham, Edward; 27 January 1812; to serve until 16

Price, William, son of Veazey Price; 20 July 1795; 16; Oldham, Edward; - ; to serve until 21

Oldham, Jacob of Joseph; 14 May 1797; 14; Graham, Zachariah, cabinetmaker; 11 February 1812; to serve until 21

Grant, Sarah of George; 28 February 1806; 5; Benjamin, George; 11 February 1812; to serve until 16

Currier, Victor, son of Jonathan Currier; 2 July 1794; 17; Gale, George, sawyer; 25 March 1812; to serve until 2 July 1815 (age 21)

Richardson, Henry; 15 February 1798; 14; Reynolds, Stephen, miller; 21 March 1812; to serve until 21

Heath, Sophia, a girl of color; - ; - ; Lightner, George; 20 April 1812; to serve a term

of seventeen years from this date
Berry, Nancy a Negro Wench; - ; - ; Lightner, George; 20 April 1812; to serve a term of 12 years from this date
King, a Negro boy; - ; - ; Thomas, Evan W.; 20 April 1812; to serve a term of 15 years from this date
William, a Negro boy; - ; - ; Thomas, Evan W.; 20 April 1812; to serve a term of 26 years from this date
John, a Negro boy; - ; - ; Thomas, Evan W.; 20 April 1812; to serve a term of 23 years from this date
Lindy, a Negro girl; - ; - ; Thomas, Evan W.; 20 April 1812; to serve a term of 16 years from this date
Cloe, a Negro girl; - ; - ; Thomas, Evan W; 20 April 1812; to serve a term of 16 years from this date
Maxwell, James, son of William Maxwell; 21 May 1796; 16; Brown, Nathan, saddler; 1 May 1812; to serve until 21 April 1817
Cope/Coope, Nathan; Chester, Pennsylvania; - ; 16; Haines, Elisha; 5 May 1812; to serve three years, six months from this date
Moore, John; - ; 18; Anderson, London, blacksmith; 9 June 1812; to serve until 21

Segars, Francis, son of Reuben; 15 February 1799; 13; Turner, George C., miller; 9 June 1812; to serve until 21
McKeaver/McCervey, William, son of William; 4 September 1796; 17; McGowan, George Jr., cordwainer; 13 August 1812; to serve until 4 July 1814
Grant, William, son of George; 28 February 1802; 10; Moffett, Thomas, Justice of the Orphan Court; 11 August 1812; to serve until 21
Riddle, Humphrey, of Levi; 22 November 1801; 10; Benjamin, George, boot & shoe maker; 11 August 1812; to serve until 21
Lewis, George, 'a black boy'; 6 June 1806; 6; Thomas, Theodore, farmer; 11 August 1812; to serve until 21
Charles,' a black boy'; 4 May 1797; 15; Gillespie, Francis, cooper; 13 August 1812; to serve until 21
Cazier, John Foard. (with the consent of his mother); 11 July 1798; 14; Billefelt, William, merchant; 19 August 1812; to serve until 19
Nugent, Samuel; 8 March 1798; 14; Johnson, Charles,

clothier; 13 September 1812; to serve until 21
Leonard, Tacey, with the consent of her mother, Tacey Leonard; - ; 7; Clements, Samuel, farmer; 4 October 1812; to serve until 16
Ringler, Catherine of Jonathan; 14 October 1800; 11; Dysart, James, hatter; 14 December 1812; to serve until 16
Ringler, William, of Jonathan; 3 September ___; - ; Dysart, James, hatter; 14 December 1812; to serve until 21
Gottier, John; 30 January 1798; 15; Rhinehold, Jacob, husbandman; 10 February 1813; to serve until 21
Bostwick, Dinah, a woman of color; - ; - ; Lightner, George W. (purchaser of her manumission ($200); 17 February 1813; to serve a term of 10 years, then free
Richard, Negro; - ; - ; Lightner, John, esq.; 23 March 1813; to serve 15 years, then free
Gibson, Thomas, son of John; 13 February 1797; 16; Brown, Montiliou, cartwright and blacksmith; 1 April 1813; to serve until 21
Morton, John H. of Jacob; 13 February 1807; 6; Davidson, John H.,

cartwright; 1 April 1813; to serve until 21
Eliza, 'a black woman'; - ; - ; Warfield, Mary; 10 April 1813; to serve 15 years, then free
McCologh, James, son of James; 4 September 1794; 18; Reynolds, Benjamin, carpenter; 10 August 1813; to serve until 21
Brown, Daniel, son of Daniel; 26 November 1795; 17; Reynolds, Benjamin, carpenter; 10 August 1813; to serve until 21
McNeal, John, son of Thomas; 14 August 1802; 10; Dysart, James, hatter; 6 March 1813; to serve until 21
Brown, Rose,'a black girl'; 1 June 1808; 5; Ramsey, William; 7 June 1813; to serve until 28
Joseph, 'a destitute black boy'; January 1799; 14; Hall, Samuel, farmer; 24 April 1813; to serve until 21
McCleary, Elizabeth of Jacob; 22 November 1803; 9; Brown, Montiliou; 7 April 1813; to serve until 16
Fanney, a black girl, with the consent of her father; - ; - ; Arthur, Mark; 23 May 1813; to serve 11 years, then free
Gwin, John, son of John; 5 January 1798; 15; Scott,

James, cartwright and blacksmith; 10 August 1813; to serve until 21

Negro George; 15 September 1807; 6; McMullen, John; 15 September 1813; to serve until 28

Morrison, Arthur; 17 February 1808; 5; Brown, Hugh, blacksmith; 7 November 1813; to serve until 21

Hawkins, James; - ; - ; Gay, Samuel, blacksmith; 8 December 1813; to serve 4 years and 2 months, then free

Leonard, John, son of William; 1 November 1804; 9; Ewing, Moses, cooper; 27 December 1813; to serve until 21

Rowls, Hezekiah, with the consent of his father, Elihu Rowls; 2 September 1795; 18; Harton, Thomas, house joiner; 28 December 1813; to serve until 21

Davis, Robert with the consent of his grandfather Daniel, McKinney; 29 March 1798; 13; Sturgeon, Thomas, taylor; 8 February 1814; to serve until 21

Hassin, John, son of Samuel; - ; - ; Reynolds, Richard B., cordwinder; 8 January 1814; to serve until 21

Knott, George Peregrine; 30 June 1804; 9; Knight,

Thomas, blacksmith; 4 December 1813; to serve until 21

Robinson, Thomas; 12 April 1805; 9; Patterson, Henry, weaver; 22 July 1814; to serve until 21

Index

BRAVARD, Joshua 15 21
BRISCOE, Samuel 12 Tobias
  12
BROOKES, John 31
BROWN, Caleb 28 Daniel 33
  David 21 28 Elisha 9 14 19
  Hugh 34 Jesse 10 John 9
  Joseph 9 Montiliou 33
  Nathan 32 Richard 19
  Robert 19 Robert Jr 29 Rose
  33 Samuel 12 William 28
BROWNE, Edmund 18
BRYAN, John 19 26 Phillip 13
BRYRGOYNE, James 29
  Richard 29
BRYSON, Thomas 20
BUCKRAM, James 15 Joseph
  28 Mary 15 Moly 28
BULLTELL, Henry Empson
  19
BULTEEL, Henry 9 Rachel 9
BURGOYNE, John 16
  Margaret 16
BURK, Nathanial 22
BURRIS, James 18
CALDW, Katherine 17
  Thomas 17
CALDWELL, Thomas 17
CALLINDEN, John 17
CALWELL, John 18
CAMERON, John 25 John Sr
  19
CAMPBELL, Ann 19 John 9
  Letitia 19 Samuel 11
CARL, Mary 17
CARR, Robert 11
CARSWELL, John 19
CARTER, James 31 Samuel 31
CARUTHERS, George 19

CASHNER, John 12
CASHORE, William 27
CATHER, Hannah 26
CATO, Josiah 28
CAZIER, John Foard 32
CHAMBERS, Nicholas 21
  Richard 13
CHANDLEE, James 23
CHANDLER, Francis B 9 13
CHAPPLE, William 14
CHREATE, John 30 Samuel 30
CHRISTE, Robert 23
CHRISTIE, James 26
CHURCHMAN, George Jr 28
CLAYTON, Andrew John 26
CLEMENT, Thomas 29
CLEMENTS, Samuel 33
COBOURN, Mary 20
COCHRAN, Robert 14 31
CONARY, Matthew 29
CONDON, Samuel 19
CONNALY, Charles 27
CONNER, James Chadick 16
CONNOR, Elinor 19
CONRAD, John 22 26
CONWAY, William 10
COOLIN, Lydia 11
COOPE, Nathan 32
COPE, Nathan 32
CORL, Mary 17
COUDON, Rachel 19
COULSON, Abner 17 George
  18
COURAD, John 21
COWAN, William 21 29
COX, Noble 28
CRACHEN, James 27
CRAWFORD, William 29

CROOKSHANKS, John 19-20
Nancy 20 William 19
CROTHERS, John 26 William
28
CROUCH, Edward 22 Sarah
22 Susanah 22
CROW, Owen 22
CROWLEY, James 13 John 11
Matthew 11 13
CSBY, Fatima 20
CULLY, George 14 George Jr
27
CUMINGS, James 27
CUMMINGS, David 29 James
26 Samuel 26
CUMMINS, James 29
CUMMNGS, David 20
CUNNINGHAM, John 17
CURRIER, Jonathan 31 Victor
31
DALRYMPLE, James 27
DAVIDSON, John H 33
DAVIS, Elizabeth 11 Robert
34 William 11 21
DAVISON, John 11 24
Margaret 10 Robert 10 16
Sussanah 10
DEAN, John 30
DEGROVE, Richard 28
DENNIS, John 19
DEVLIN, John 29
DICK, Samuel 21
DICKEY, Jane 26
DICKSON, Andrew 17 James
26
DIXON, Mary 18
DOLAN, James 30 Thomas 24
30
DONALD, James B 20

DUNBAR, Andrew 28
DUNCAN, Hannah 13 John 9
DUNKEN, Samuel 27
DUNLAP, Lucretia 16
DYSART, James 33
EDMISTON, David 10
EDMONDSON, James 14
EDMONSON, Blaney 14
EDMUNDSON, Blany 15
Caleb 26
ELI, Cameron 31 James 31
ELLIOTT, Benjamin 29 Henry
29 Jesse 29
ENGLAND, Elisha 12 Isaac 31
John 10
ERVIN, Jane 19
ERWIN, Jane 19
EVAN, W Thomas 30
EVANS, James 11 Samuel 12
William 27 30
EWING, Henry 20 John 16
Moses 34 Putnam 18 Robert
11
FERGERSON, Jesse 30
Zebulon 30
FERRILL, James 29
FOARD, John H 20
FORD, Bettey 12
FORT, Juliet 12
FOX, John 14
FRENCH, James 20 James
Ross 20 Samuel 20
FULTON, James 28 Thomas
30 William 31
GALE, George 31
GALLIHER, Abraham 13
GALLOWAY, John 22 Robert
22

GARRETT, Sarah 26 Thomas
26 30 Thomas Jr 26
William 28
GARRETTT, Samuel 30
William 30
GATCHEL, Elisha 21
GATCHELL, Elisha 28
GAY, Samuel 19 34 Samuel Jr
22 30
GEORGE, Sidney 11 16
GERRY, James 31
GIBBONS, John 26
GIBBONY, Ann 26
GIBSON, Elizabeth 19 John 33
Thomas 33
GILBEATH, James 9 William
9
GILLELAND, Thomas 16
GILLESPIE, Francis 32
Samuel 13
GILLSEPIE, Jane 31
GILPIN, Samuel 14
GINN, John 21
GLEENN, Joannes 10
GLENN, Samuel Jr 10
GOLDEN, Jonathan 29
GORRELL, Archibald 25
GOTTIER, John 33
GRAHAM, William 19
Zachariah 31
GRAISH, Edward 19
GRANT, David 26 George 31-
32 Sarah 31 William 32
GREEN, Edward 15
GREENLAND, Abner 15
GWIN, John 33
HAINES, Eli 15 18 31 Elisha
32 Job Jr 24 Reuben 15
Thomas 17

HAINS, Eli 29
HALL, Isaac 13 James 16 20
John 15 Lewis Gray 24
Richard 23 Samuel 33
HAMILTON, George 11
HAMMOND, John 10 Poll 10
HANCE, James 15
HANDSHAW, Amos 21
HANER, Elizabeth 26 Hyland
26
HANNA, Richard 20
HANNAH, Joseph 27 Samuel
27
HARGEN, Eli 25
HARLAN, Joseph 20 31
HARRIDGE, Mary 9 Samuel 9
HARTSHORN, John 11 Nancy
25
HARTSHOWN, Agnes 13
HASSIN, John 34 Samuel 34
HAVEY, Ann 13
HAWKINS, James 34
HEATH, Richard Key 14
Sophia 31
HEDHAM, John 12
HEGAN, Catherine 11 James
11
HENDERSON, David 28
HENDRICKS, Elizabeth 9
Jacob 9
HILL, George 12 James 15   .
Joseph 14
HINDMAN, Mary 20
HODGSON, James 12 17 27
HOLLIDAY, James 30 John 30
HOLLINGSWORTH, Henry
10 13-15 John 18 William
20

HOLMES, George 18 William 18
HOLT, Jesse 22 Joseph 22
HOLTON, Benjamin 14
HOPKINS, John 15 Joseph 15
HOWARD, Thomas 21 24-25 31 William 12 16 18
HUGG, Richard 16
HUGGINS, Mary 9 Samuel 9
HUGHES, Edward 26 James 26 Joseph 20
HUKIN, Elijah 21
HULL, Ann M 30 John 31
HUME, William 22
HUMES, Agnes 22
HUSLAR, John 20
HUSLER, John 11 22
HYATT, Abraham 10
HYLAND, John 28
HYNSON, Thomas 14-15 20
IRWIN, Abner 25 James 28 Jesse 25 John 25
JACKSON, Henry 9 James 15 John 21 23 Peter 11
JARRETT, Elisha 18
JEMMAR, Patrick Henry 16
JENKINS, Rachel 28
JOB, Daniel Jr 13
JOHN, Robert 25 31
JOHNSON, Charles 12 16 32 David 13 Jonathan 12
JOHNSTON, George 22
JONES, Edward J 25 James 17 21 Richard 10 William 11-12
JORDAN, Jane 20 John 13 21 William 20
KARSHNER, Daniel 29
KARTNER, Daniel 24

KASSNER, David 23
KEAN, John 17
KELLY, Thomas 18
KENNEDY, George 25 John 23 Moses 23
KERTIKART, Molly 23
KESLER, John 24
KE_IHAN, Molly 23
KIDD, Charles 29
KIDMAN, Mary 19
KILLPATRICK, John 21
KINKEAD, William 25
KIRK, John 28 William 11
KIRKILL, John 24 Joseph 24
KIRKPATRICK, James 13
KNIGHT, Azor 29 John 25 Thomas 34
KNOTT, George Peregrine 34 James 10 William 10
KUISLER, William 17
LACKLAND, Samuel 21
LAIRD, Miller 27
LANCASTER, Isaac 11
LASHLEY, Thomas 10
LAWS, Robert 28
LECKY, Thomas 15
LEE, Elias 12
LEECH, Robert 17 William 16
LEMMON, Archibald 16
LEONARD, Elizabeth 29 James 34 John 28 Mary 28 Tacey 33 William 34
LEWIS, Anne 22 Robert 30
LIGHTNER, George 31-32 George W 33 John 33
LOCKWOOD, George 29
LOGUN, Thomas 23
LONG, Elizabeth 13 Hannah 13 John 19 23 Robert 13

LONGWELL, Robert 20
LOUTTIT, Henry 22
LOWE, John 17 Levi 11
LOWREY, Rebecca 26
    Rebeccah 23
LOWRY, James 14
LOWS, Robert 28
LUEENS, Mary 24
LYNCH, William 12
MACKEY, William Beard 22
MAFFITT, Samuel 22
MAGEE, James 9
MAGRAW, James 25
MANSFIELD, Richard 11
MARSHALL, Isaac L 31
    James 29
MARTIN, Hester 10
MASSITT, Samuel 22
MATTHEWS, Jane 22 John 13
    Joseph 11 Robert 22
MAXWELL, James 18 32
    William 32
MCBRIDE, Bendict 11 James
    13
MCCARDLE, James 19 John
    19
MCCARLIN, Robert 15
MCCASLIN, Robert 19
MCCERVEY, William 32
MCCLEARY, Elizabeth 33
MCCOLOGH, James 33
MCCORKLE, James A 23
MCCOY, Alexander 15 John
    16 John H 24 Joseph 15
MCCRAEKIN, John 27
MCCRAKEN, John 24
MCCRAKIN, James 9 12 John
    17 Thomas Blair 9
MCCRERY, John 13

MCCULLOGH, Alexander 14
    Andrew 14 John 18
MCCULLY, John 27
MCDOWELL, Eavan 24
    Nancy 24 Robert 27 Samuel
    23 Thomas 24 William 19
MCELWEE, Samuel 18
MCGARITY, Ann 12
MCGOWAN, George Jr 32
MCGOWEN, John 29
MCGRADY, John 9-10
MCGRAW, William 12
MCGREATH, William 11
MCKEAVER, Charles M 23
    Thomas 23 William 32
MCKEVER, Alexander 23
MCKINLEY, Lucretia 17
MCKINNEY, Daniel 34
MCKRAKEN, John 26
MCLAUGHLIN, Mary 13
MCMILLUN, James 18
MCMULLEN, John 33
    Thomas 18
MCMULLIN, Robert 18
MCNEAL, John 33 Thomas 33
MCQUE, Dominick 31 Mary
    31
MCVEY, Benjamin 17 Joshua
    Davis 25
MEEKINS, Richard 24
MERRYMAN, John 23
MIFFLIN, John 16
MILES, Isaac 9
MILLER, Lewis 11-12 15 18
    21 24 Samuel 11 19
    William 13
MILLS, John 9 Robert 9
MITTER, Samuel 9
MITTES, Samuel 9

MOFFETT, Thomas 32
MONEY, Eleanor 10 Hyland 9
    Robert 9 Thomas 10 13
MOODY, David 21 Isaac 21
MOORE, Alexander 17 27
    Eloner 24 George 9 20 John
    32 Joseph 15 Moses 26
    Sarah 25 William 16
    William C 21
MORGAN, Thomas 25
MORRISON, Arthur 34
    Rebeccah 21
MORTON, John H 33
MULATTO, Charles 21
MURPHY, Margaret 17
    Stephen 20
MURRAN, Susannah 22
NEAL, John 23 Joseph 23
    Rebeccah 12
NEGRO, Abigal 9 Abraham 18
    Catherine 30 Charles 32
    Cloe 32 Eliza 33 Fanny 33
    George 30 33 Jacob 28
    James 31 John 32 Joseph 33
    Judith 9 Julianna 26 King
    32 Lindy 32 Ninian 16
    Phillis 30 Richard 33 Sarah
    18 30 Thom 13 20 Tom 30
    William 28
NISBETT, Joseph Gordon 25
NISBITT, Alexander 25
NOWLAND, Benedict 13
NUGENT, Samuel 32
OLDHAM, Edward 31 Jacob
    31 Joseph 31 Nathanial 22
    Richard 9
ORRICK, Hannah 18 James 18
OWEINGS, Rachael 25
OWENS, Thomas 10

OWINGS, Ruth 25
PARQUET, Marcellus William
    29
PARRY, David 9-10 Jesse 10
    Sarah 9
PARSLEY, Mary 14
PARTRIDGE, James 15 17
PATTEN, John 22 Sophia 14
    Thomas 14 16 21 23-24 26
    30
PATTER, John 23
PATTERSON, Henry 34 Jane
    23 William 23
PATTON, John 18 Thomas 25
PAXSON, Anne 24 Charles 24
PEARCE, Benjamin 30 Henry
    Ward 11 William 18
PEDEN, Elizabeth 12 Hugh 12
PEERY, William 29
PENNINGTON, Elias 11 Isaac
    9 John 12 25 Joseph 17
    Sarah 12 William 9 William
    Canby 12
PERRY, Israel 17
PHILLIPS, Joseph 27 Nancy
    27 Nicholas 11 Samuel 11
    Zebulon 20
PLYMOUTH, Ben 27 Susan
    27
POND, Lambert 26
PORPER, James 22
PORTER, John 19 29
POWLEY, John 26 Thomas 26
PRESTON, William 14
PRICE, Ann 27 Catherine 24
    Elizabeth 31 James N 16
    John H 21 John N 27 29
    Joshua 19 Thomas 27
    Veazey 31 William 31

PRICER, John Hyland 20
PRITCHARD, Carvil 14 James
22
PRITCHET, Amos 11
PUGH, James 21 Joseph 22
QUAIL, Elizabeth 21
QUIN, George 24 John 24
RABB, John 24
RALSTON, Joseph 19
RAMSEY, James 16 Samuel
25 31 William 33
RATLIFF, James 16 18 21
REA, Catherine 14
REALY, Isaac 26 William 26
REED, Charles 24
REESE, Matilda 17
REEVES, Robert 21
REGEN, James 23 Rachel 23
REYNODLS, Thomas 11
REYNODS, Stephen 20
REYNOLDS, Benjamin 25 30
33 Elizabeth 23 Henry 30
Jacob 29 John 21 Jonathan
13-14 17 23 Joshua 30
Richard 17 Richard B 34
Samuel 13 15 Stephen 25
31 Thomas 27 29 William
28
RHINEHOLD, Jacob 33
RICE, George 25
RICHARDSON, Henry 31
Thomas 31
RICKETS, George 18 John 24
RICKETTS, William 25
RIDDLE, Humphrey 32
RINGLER, Catherine 33 John
28 Jonathan 28 33 William
33
RITCHIE, James 25 Jesse 25

ROBB, Anthony 29 Levi 29
ROBERT, John 25
ROBINSON, Henry 16
Thomas 34
RODGERS, Rowland 19
ROGERS, Catherine 15
Thomas 12 16 19 25
William 28
RONEY, Sarah 18
ROSLS, Elihu 34
ROSS, John 17
ROWLS, Elihu 17 Hezekiah 34
RULEY, James Henry 28
RUTTER, Margary 21 Moses
12 18 Samuel 12 Thomas
12 22
RYLAND, Peter 9 Sussanah 27
SAMPLE, John 20
SCHILTREE, Matthews 20
SCOTT, James 26 33 Moses 27
30 Thomas 27
SCRIVAN, George 12
SEAGER, Josiah 14
SEGARS, Francis 32 Reuben
32
SEVERSON, Hance 14
SHAFFER, James 20
SHARPE, John 9
SHATTACH, Levi 16
SHAW, John 10
SHEPPARD, David 22
SHURMIZER, Jacob 12
SIMPSON, Richard 11
SIPPLES, Henry 24 Susannah
24
SLICER, John 16
SMITH, David 19 24 Delia 16
Hannah 16 Henry 12 18

Joseph 23 Richard 14
Steward 27
SPARROWGROW, John 9
Lydia 9
SPRINGER, Mary Ann 17
Peter 18
STANDISH, Miles 23
STEDHAM, Henry 12
STEPHENSON, David 13
STEVENSON, David 14 John
19
STURGEON, Thomas 34
SULLIVAN, Aaron 26
Elizabeth 26 Nathan 28
Rebecca 10 William 10 19
SUTTON, Jock 15
SWEANY, David 15
TAGGERT, Peter 17
TANNER, Joseph 13
TAYLOR, John 27 Joseph 22
Luke 27 Noble 18 Robert
20 Samuel 30 Thomas 16
18
TERY, William 9
THOM, Jean 13
THOMAS, Evan W 30 32
Isaac 12 Mary 12 Theodore
32
THOMPSON, John 20 Mary
15 Robert 24 26 William 10
15 17
THRIETH, James 21
TODD, Levi 31 Margaret 31
William 31
TOLAND, Joshua 11
TOLBUM, Deborah 12
TONY, Millie 22
TURNER, George C 32

TWEEDY, David 18 James 17
Susannah 17
TYLON, Isaac 17
TYSON, Levi 17
UNDERGROVES, Richard 27
VEAZEY, Benoni 28
WALKER, John 13 30
WALLACE, James 22 Michael
9 12 Samuel Patterson 15
WALLASTON, Joseph 29
WALMSLEY, Robert 12
William 13
WALSH, William 20
WARD, John 13 Samuel 15
Thomas 15
WARE, William 18
WARFIELD, Mary 33
WATT, James 11 John 11
WATTS, Catherine 10 Samuel
10
WELCH, Elizabeth 16 John 14
Robert 16 Sarah 14
WELSH, Jenny 11 William 11
WHAN, Sally 9
WHITE, Abner 20 Jacob 15
John 20 Katherine 20 Levi
11 Thomas 18 25 William
20
WHITELOCK, James 15
WHITTAKER, Ralph 16
William 16
WICKES, James 19
WILKINSON, Robert 16 23-24
WILLCOCKS, William 23
WILLIAM, Elizabeth 24
Howard 24
WILLIAMS, Basil 21
Elizabeth 14 Jesse 22
Margaret 14 Thomas 21

WILLSON, Darcus 21 Mary 15
  William 19
WILSON, Elizabeth 13 Isaac
  10 John 31 Levina 17 19
  Margaret 15
WIMBLE, John 21 Joseph 29
WINCHESTER, 27 Ann 10
  Timothy 10 27 William 10
WIRT, Jacob 11 John 11
WOOD, John 30 Samuel 25
  Thomas 25

WORK, Samuel 24 William 24
WRIGHT, Abraham 30 David
  14 Margaret 13 Thomas 9
WYNCOOP, Abraham 9
YEOMAN, Elizabeth 22 John
  22
YORK, Benjamin 28
YOUNG, William 16
YOUNGER, Hannah 9 James 9